Little bear's
Colours

Little Bear's
Colours

JANE HISSEY

RED FOX

red orange yellow green blue

red balloon

purple pink brown black white

Bramwell has given Jolly a long **red** scarf.

orange yellow green blue purple

orange pumpkin

pink brown black white red

Jolly is painting with orange paint.

yellow **wool**

brown **black** white red orange

Hoot is sharing her yellow cheese.

green blue purple pink brown

green umbrella

black white red orange yellow

What is the green monkey eating?

blue purple pink brown black

blue bone

Little Bear is standing on a blue chair.

purple pink brown black white

purple hat

red orange yellow green blue

Jolly has caught two **purple** balloons.

pink brown **black** white red

pink blanket

orange yellow green blue purple

Lizzie Long Ears is wearing a pink dress.

brown black white red orange

brown monkey

The bears are cosy in their **brown** basket.

black white red orange yellow

black cat

green blue purple pink brown

The **black** dog is hiding his rubber bones.

white  red orange yellow green

white box

blue purple pink brown **black**

Old Bear is cutting out white decorations.

stripes

black and white **stripes**

Can you find the **stripy** socks?

spots

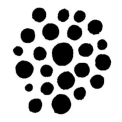

black spots

How many **spotty** things can you see?

checks

checked bow

Little Bear's boat has a **checked** sail.

Which **colours** and **patterns**
can you find?

For Richard, Karen and Rowena

LITTLE BEAR'S COLOURS
A RED FOX BOOK 0 09 943394 X

First published in Great Britain by Hutchinson,
an imprint of Random House Children's Books

Hutchinson edition published 2002
Red Fox edition published 2003

1 3 5 7 9 10 8 6 4 2

Red Fox Books are published by Random House Children's Books,
61–63 Uxbridge Road, London W5 5SA,
a division of The Random House Group Ltd,
in Australia by Random House Australia (Pty) Ltd,
20 Alfred Street, Milsons Point, Sydney, NSW 2061, Australia,
in New Zealand by Random House New Zealand Ltd,
18 Poland Road, Glenfield, Auckland 10, New Zealand,
and in South Africa by Random House (Pty) Ltd,
Endulini, 5A Jubilee Road, Parktown 2193, South Africa

THE RANDOM HOUSE GROUP Limited Reg. No. 954009
www.kidsatrandomhouse.co.uk

A CIP catalogue record for this book is available from the British Library.

Printed in Singapore